MW00817088

101 DELAWARE WING-T DRILLS

Harold R. "Tubby" Raymond
Ted Kempski

COACHES CHOICE

ISBN: 1-57167-162-5
Library of Congress Catalog Card Number: 97-80944

Cover Design and Diagrams: Deborah M. Bellaire
Front Cover Photo: Max Gretsch
Developmental Editor: Joanna Wright
Production Manager: Michelle A. Summers

Coaches Choice Books is an division of: Sagamore Publishing, Inc.
P.O. Box 647
Champaign, IL 61824-0647
Web Site: http//www.sagamorepub.com

DEDICATION

This book is dedicated to all the fine young men who established the football tradition and played for us at the University of Delaware.

ACKNOWLEDGMENTS

We are deeply indebted to the coaches who taught football with us during my tenure as head football coach at the University of Delaware.

Marty Apostolico	Ted Kempski
Herky Billings	Otto Kneidinger
Paul Billy	David Lockwood
Bryan Bossard	Jeff Lukas
Tom Coder	Ed Maley
David Cohen	Josh Mastrangelo
Tony DeMeo	Jim McCarthy
Bob Depew	Mike Miller
Kevin Dickerson	Gregg Perry
Mike DiMartile	Joe Purzycki
R.B. "Scotty" Duncan	Chris Raymond
Jimmy Flynn	Ron Rogerson
Tony Glenn	Warren Ruggerio
Ted Gregory	Bob Sabol
Jim Grube	Greg Ventresca
Marshall Hall	Steve Verbit
Eric Hammack	Matt Wildes
Don Harnum	Irvin Wisniewski
Mickey Heinecken	Bob Wolford

CONTENTS

We wrote this series of five books, *The Delaware Wing-T: The Running Game, The Option Game and the Passing Game, 101 Delaware Wing-T Drills,* and *101 Delaware Wing-T Plays* to provide coaches at all competitive levels with tools to enable them to better understand and implement the Delaware Wing-T. Each volume is designed to complement the other four books.

Volume 1 examines how to institute an effective running game with the Delaware Wing-T offense. Volumes 2 and 3 present an overview of how we employ an option attack and a passing attack, respectively, from the Delaware Wing-T. Volume 4 provides 101 drills for developing, practicing and refining the various essential fundamentals and techniques that are integral to the Delaware Wing-T. Finally, Volume 5 includes 101 basic plays that can be incorporated into a Delaware Wing-T offensive system.

Collectively, we hope that these books will provide you with the insights, the information and the foundation needed to fully comprehend and utilize the Delaware Wing-T. Properly executed, this unique offense can enable you to take advantage of your players' specific talents and skills in a goal-oriented, creative way.

Football is a great game. As a metaphor for life, football involves many of the critical elements that are required for success in almost any undertaking—sacrifice, hard work, teamwork, planning and an unrelenting commitment to excellence. To the extent that this series of five books (and a companion series of five instructional videos) enables you—in some small way—to appreciate this terrific game even more, then our efforts to write these volumes and to produce these videos will have been well worthwhile.

Harold R. "Tubby" Raymond
Ted Kempski

CHAPTER 1

QUARTERBACK DRILLS

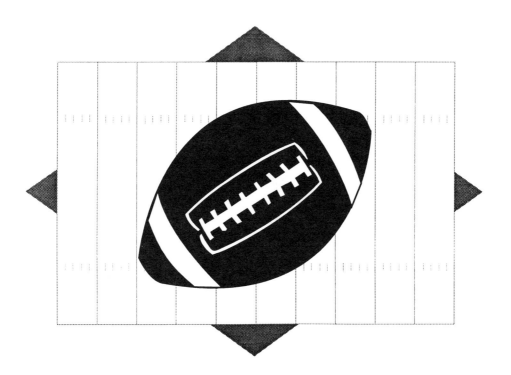

Drill #1: Pitch Warm-Up Drill

Objective: To warm up; to practice pitching the ball.

Equipment Needed: Footballs.

Description: Two quarterbacks face each other, approximately five yards apart. They should be offset so their right hands are in line with each other. They should pitch the ball to each other with their right hands, then move so their left hands are aligned and pitch with their left hands. To pitch the ball properly, the quarterback holds the ball in a passing grip, then turns his hand under and flips the ball as he steps toward the target. The pitch should be aimed just above the numbers.

Coaching Points:

- The coach should observe the quarterbacks' pitching technique and make corrections when necessary.

- The coach should stress the importance of keeping the pitch number high to avoid a low pitch.

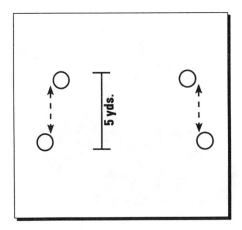

Drill #2: SPR 121 Trap Option—SPR 929 Trap Option

Objective: To practice the SPR 121 (or 929) Trap Option

Equipment Needed: Two line spacing tapes, four cones, footballs.

Description: The two tapes are placed near the center of the field. A center, quarterback, and fullback line up at each station. The left halfbacks line up on the right side of the field and vice versa. A cone is placed at the outside end of each tape to represent the inside foot of the 3 man and designate the pitch point. Another cone is placed five yards outside the tape and two yards behind the line of scrimmage to designate where the ball should be caught. The quarterback calls cadence and receives the snap, and then he and the halfback execute the pitch.

Coaching Point:

- The coach should emphasize the importance of the correct timing and placement of the pitch.

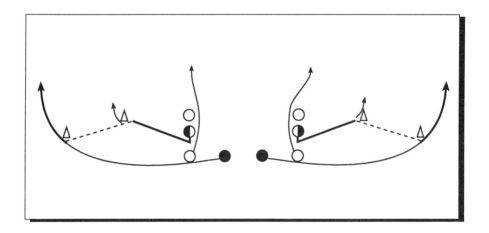

Drill #3: 981 Option—189 Option (Belly Option)

Objective: To practice the 981 (or 189) Option.

Equipment Needed: Two line spacing tapes, four cones, footballs.

Description: The equipment and personnel are aligned in the same manner as in the SPR 121 Trap Option drill, except the halfbacks are moved to the wing positions. The quarterback and fullback execute their 82 Down technique. The halfback must leave in one step motion to be in place to catch the pitch.

Coaching Point:

- The coach should emphasize the importance of the correct timing and placement of the pitch and the timely arrival of the halfback.

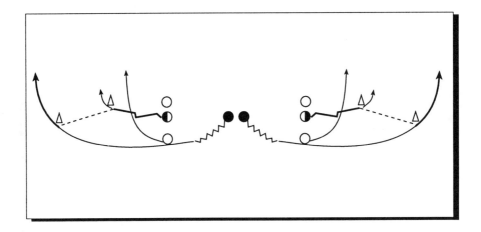

Drill #4: 991 Option—199 Option (Lead Option)

Objective: To practice the 991 (or 199) Option.

Equipment Needed: Two line spacing tapes, four cones, footballs.

Description: The equipment is positioned in the same manner as in the Trap Option drill. The only difference in the personnel alignment is that the halfbacks switch sides of the field (i.e., the right halfbacks should be on the right side). When executing this play, the fullback is the pitch man and the halfback performs an arc block on 4.

Coaching Points:

- The coach should emphasize the importance of the correct timing and placement of the pitch.

- The coach should critique the halfback's blocking technique.

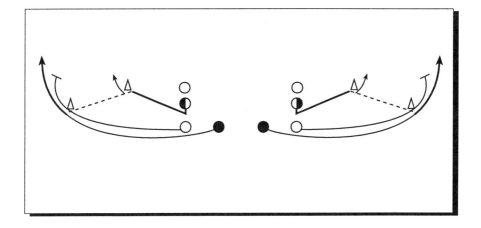

Drill #5: Warm-up Progression

Objective: To warm up; to practice various passing techniques.

Equipment Needed: Footballs.

Description: Two quarterbacks face each other at a distance of 10 yards and pass the ball back and forth. After they have loosened up, they increase the distance to 15 yards. As they continue to throw, they should focus on their releases and throwing the ball to a specific spot (i.e., the right shoulder). The quarterbacks should next simulate moving parallel to the line of scrimmage by facing the sideline and moving along it. During this phase of the drill the quarterbacks should concentrate on rotating their upper body so their shoulders are square to the target when the ball is released. In the final phase of the drill, the quarterbacks throw on the run. The player with the ball runs at his partner, who maintains the 15-yard separation by backpedaling.

Coaching Points:

- The coach should emphasize getting on top of the ball to ensure a live release.

- The coach should stress the importance of proper mechanics throughout this drill.

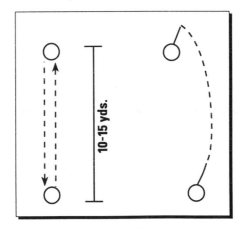

Drill #6: Sprint Out Drill

Objective: To improve a quarterback's ability to throw on the run.

Equipment Needed: Four cones, footballs.

Description: Cones are placed on opposite hash marks 15 yards apart. Two quarterbacks are lined up at each cone. Two more cones are set up to represent the inside foot of the halfback. The drill is run to the right and then, by changing hashes, to the left. The quarterback sprints around the cone at the halfback position, runs directly at the opposite quarterback, and passes the ball.

Coaching Point:

- The coach should make sure the quarterback is using the proper techniques when throwing on the run.

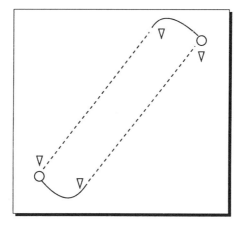

Drill #7: Dropback Drill

Objective: To practice the mechanics of the quarterback's drop.

Equipment Needed: Footballs.

Description: Four quarterbacks line up a yard apart from each other along the line of scrimmage. A tight end and wingback are aligned on the right, while a split end and diveback are positioned on the left. Each quarterback takes a five-or-seven step drop, depending on the pattern his designated receiver is running, and makes the pass. One of the best combinations is for the tight end and wingback to run a hook and flat combination on the right while the split end and diveback run a curl and flare combination to the left. Halfway through the drill, the four receivers switch sides.

Coaching Points:

- The coach should emphasize proper dropback and passing mechanics.

- The coach should rotate receivers in during the drill.

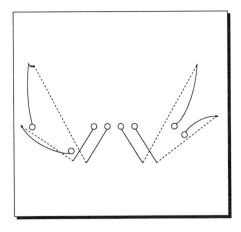

Drill #8: Belly Keep Pass Drill

Objective: To practicing faking and throwing on the run.

Equipment Needed: Footballs, two cones.

Description: Two quarterbacks line up two yards apart with a fullback behind each. The tight end and wingback line up on the right side, with the split end and diveback on the left. A cone is placed at the inside foot of each dive position. The quarterback should fake the handoff, then run around the cone and directly at the target to make the pass.

Coaching Points:

- The receivers change sides halfway through the drill.

- The quarterback should immediately get a passing grip on the ball so he is prepared to throw quickly as he comes off the fake.

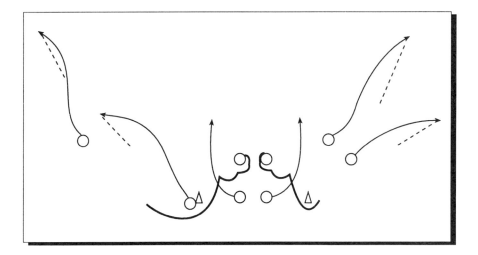

Drill #9: Backfield Timing

Objective: To practice quarterback-ballcarrier exchanges.

Equipment Needed: Two line spacing tapes, footballs.

Description: The two tapes are laid out parallel to each other 10-12 yards apart. The coach designates the play to be run, and an offensive backfield lines up behind each tape. One of the quarterbacks calls cadence, and the players perform the designated play action and exchange.

Coaching Points:

- The coach should emphasize practicing the quarterback-ballcarrier exchange with the proper timing for the called play.

- A center may be added to practice the center-quarterback exchange during the same drill.

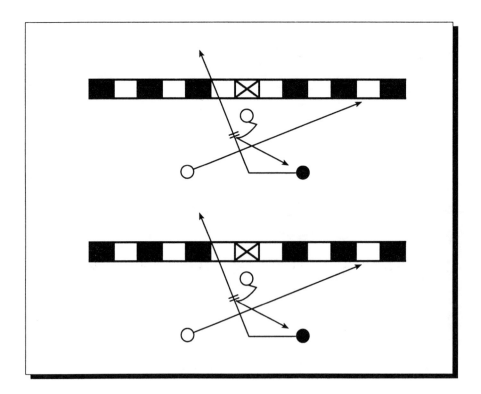

Drill #10: Blind Snap Drill

Objective: To practice the center-quarterback exchange.

Equipment Needed: Footballs.

Description: Center-quarterback pairs assume their proper exchange positions on a designated line of scrimmage. The quarterbacks close their eyes and receive snaps from the centers. The snaps should all be surprises to the quarterbacks, forcing them to react to the ball; therefore, no cadence is used. The drill should continue for 30-60 seconds.

Coaching Points:

- The centers and quarterbacks should execute their post-snap steps.

- The coach should emphasize proper exchange techniques.

Drill #11: Situational Snapping

Objective: To practice snaps used in various situations.

Equipment Needed: Footballs.

Description: The center and quarterback assume their proper exchange positions. They then practice various snaps as directed by the coach: for example, the "goose" snap, audible snaps, long count snaps, early snaps, or wet ball snaps.

Coaching Points:

- The coach should emphasize proper exchange techniques.

- The coach should vary the sequence of the snaps practiced whenever this drill is conducted.

- Any situational snap that might arise should be practiced using this drill.

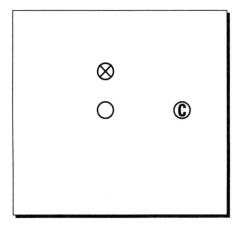

Drill #12: Deep Pass Drill

Objective: To practice and improve the quarterback's deep passing skills.

Equipment Needed: Footballs.

Description: This drill can be run using just the center, quarterback, and receiver, or with complete offensive and defensive units. The quarterback receives the snap, uses whatever methods the coach teaches to execute a deep pass (timing, reading the coverage, etc.), and passes to a receiver running a deep route designated by the coach.

Coaching Points:

- The coach may increase the level of defensive intensity and contact as the season progresses.

- The coach should emphasize using the appropriate methods to execute the deep pass and check all aspects of the quarterback's mechanics.

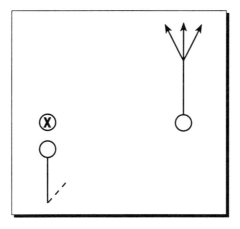

Drill #13: Pass Scrimmage

Objective: To practice the entire pass offense.

Equipment Needed: One line spacing tape, footballs.

Description: This drill involves the offensive center, backfield, and ends, and the defensive secondary, linebackers, and ends. The players line up on the appropriate side of the tape with the defenders in whichever alignment the coach chooses. The offense snaps the ball and practices all of its pass plays.

Coaching Points:

- The coach should emphasize proper timing and mechanics.

- Competition may be added to the drill by awarding points to the offense for completions and to the defense for interceptions, incompletions, or knocked-down passes.

- As the season progresses, the coach may choose to add the rest of the offensive and defensive linemen to the drill.

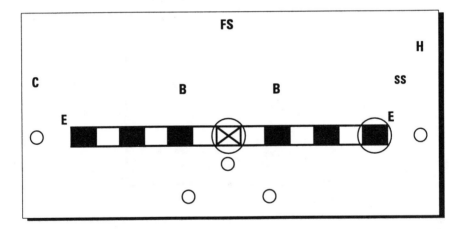

Drill #14: Read the Receiver Drill

Objective: To practice passing and reading the open receiver.

Equipment Needed: Footballs.

Description: A center and quarterback are positioned at the midpoint of a designated line of scrimmage. A receiver is placed on each hash mark eight yards in front of the line of scrimmage, and a third receiver is positioned ten yards in front of the center. The quarterback calls the play, receives the snap, and begins his drop. The coach, positioned behind and to the blind side of the quarterback, signals one of the receivers, who then flashes his hand across his chest. The quarterback sees the signal and passes to that receiver.

Coaching Points:

- The coach should emphasize using the proper mechanics and reading all three receivers.

- The drill should also be run from either hash mark, with the receivers' positions adjusted accordingly.

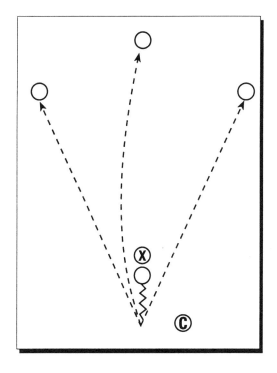

Drill #15: Multiple Snap Drill

Objective: To practice the center-quarterback exchange.

Equipment Needed: Large blocking dummies, footballs.

Description: Center-quarterback pairs are spaced five yards apart on a designated line of scrimmage. A player holding a blocking dummy is positioned over each center. One quarterback selects a play and calls cadence. The centers snap the ball and all players execute their post-snap steps.

Coaching Points:

- The coach should emphasize the proper techniques and mechanics of the exchange, making corrections when necessary.

- The drill should be performed at full speed.

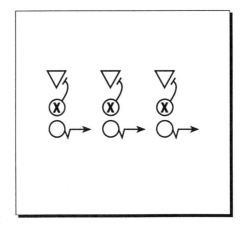

Drill #16: Kneeling Pass Drill

Objective: To practice the throwing action of the upper body.

Equipment Needed: Footballs.

Description: Two quarterbacks kneel on both knees 8-10 yards apart. They throw passes to each other, focusing on leading the arm with the chest and following through properly. The quarterbacks can also perform the drill from one knee, putting the knee opposite the throwing arm on the ground. This drill may also be used as a warm-up drill.

Coaching Point:

- The coach should stress leading the throwing arm with the chest. This motion adds the proper thrust to the pass.

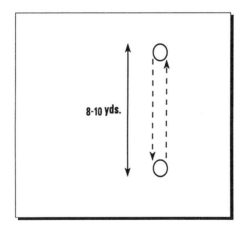

Drill #17: Turn to Throw Drill

Objective: To develop proper upper-body throwing action.

Equipment Needed: Footballs.

Description: Two quarterbacks line up 10-12 yards apart. Before passing, they turn their feet at various angles to the straight line between them and their partner. When throwing the pass, the quarterback should turn his upper body to face his partner.

Coaching Points:

- The coaches should observe the quarterbacks to make sure they are turning their upper bodies to face their partner when passing.

- The angle of the feet should change with each pass.

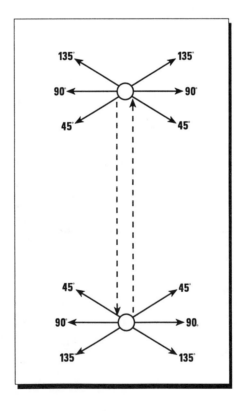

Drill #18: Quarterback Footwork Drill

Objective: To improve a quarterback's footwork.

Equipment Needed: Footballs.

Description: The quarterback sets up to throw the ball, cocking his shoulder. A receiver runs a random crossing pattern in front of him. As the receiver runs his pattern, the quarterback moves his feet and adjusts his target spot so the ball will reach the receiver at the correct point. At the coach's whistle, the quarterback should already have his feet set so he can deliver the ball to the target.

Coaching Points:

- The coach should vary the timing of the whistle to maintain the emphasis on good footwork.

- The coach may have the quarterback throw the ball immediately when he hears the whistle to check the accuracy of his setup.

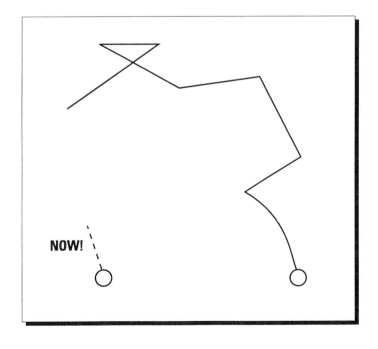

Drill #19: Step Angle Drill

Objective: To practice stepping at the proper angle to throw to a specific receiver.

Equipment Needed: Footballs.

Description: A center and quarterback are positioned on a designated line of scrimmage, and receivers are positioned at the ends of specified routes. The quarterback calls cadence, receives the snap, and takes the appropriate drop. The coach signals a receiver, who raises his hand, and the quarterback passes the ball to that player. The drill continues for a prescribed number of plays.

Coaching Points:

- The coach should emphasize the read progression and make sure the quarterback steps at the proper angle when throwing the ball.

- The drill can be run from the middle of the field or from either hash mark.

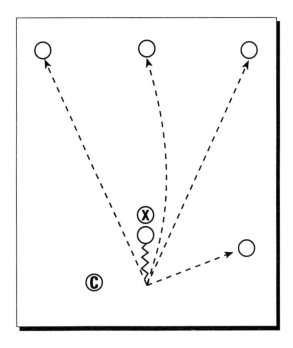

Drill #20: Handoff Drill

Objective: To practice handling and faking the football.

Equipment Needed: One line spacing tape, footballs.

Description: The quarterback, running backs, and ends are all positioned relative to the tape. The quarterback assumes his pre-snap position with a ball in each hand and calls out the play to be run. He calls cadence and takes his post-snap steps, then hands one ball off to the first running back. After this handoff, the quarterback can either hand the second ball off to the second running back or fake a second handoff and throw to one of the ends running a pass route. The drill continues for a prescribed number of plays.

Coaching Points:

- The coach should check the players' alignment and stances and make corrections where necessary.

- The coach should emphasize proper mechanics and technique in the handoff, fake, and pass.

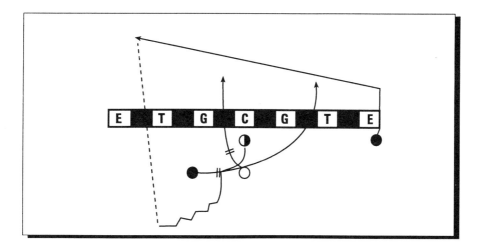

CHAPTER 2

RUNNING BACK DRILLS

Drill #21: Pivot Drill

Objective: To teach running backs to accelerate into and through contact while protecting the ball.

Equipment Needed: Six large blocking dummies, footballs.

Description: The blocking dummies are spaced five yards apart in a diagonal pattern. The running back keeps the ball in the same hand throughout the drill. He sprints five yards and explodes into the first dummy with his inside shoulder, then rolls off that shoulder and sprints for the next dummy, where he repeats the maneuver.

Coaching Points:

- The coach should emphasize accelerating into the contact with the dummies.

- The coach should stress using proper ball protection techniques.

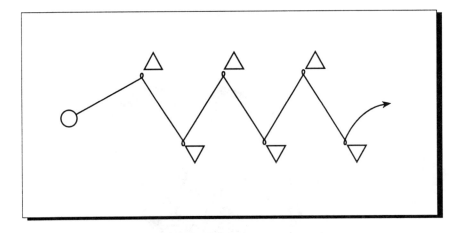

Drill #22: Serpentine Drill

Objective: To teach running backs to keep the ball tight to their body while making a move.

Equipment Needed: Six large blocking dummies, footballs.

Description: The dummies are set up in a straight line five yards apart. The running back should keep the ball in the same hand throughout the drill. He runs a serpentine path through the dummies, keeping the ball tight to his body.

Coaching Points:

- The drill should be run at full speed.

- The coach should make sure the player does not swing the ball out away from his body while weaving through the dummies.

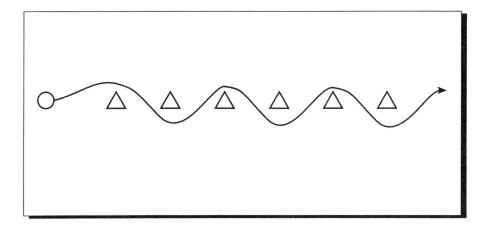

Drill #23: Safety Angles

Objective: To teach running backs to cut sharply upfield if the defensive back overruns the play.

Equipment Needed: Two cones, one line spacing tape, footballs.

Description: The left halfback takes his proper position relative to the line spacing tape. A safety lines up five yards deep over the right guard position. One cone is set up to mark the outside foot of the right end, and a second cones is set up ten yards wide of the end on the line of scrimmage. The left halfback runs around the right end at full speed, trying to force the safety to open up to contain him. If that happens, the halfback cuts sharply upfield inside the defender.

Coaching Point:

- The drill must be run at full speed to get the safety to overrun the play.

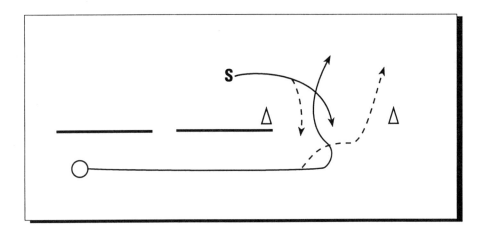

Drill #24: Pile-Up Drill

Objective: To practice diving over a pile of blockers and defenders.

Equipment Needed: Four large blocking dummies, a high jump pit, footballs.

Description: The blocking dummies are set up in front of the high jump pit. The quarterback makes a deep handoff to the running back, who makes an explosive start toward the "pile." He should gather his feet 1-1.5 yards in front of the pile, take a two-footed jump, and launch himself over the top, thrusting his upper body forward.

Coaching Points:

- The running back should have the ball secured before taking his jump.

- The players should practice various types of handoffs and approach the pile from different angles.

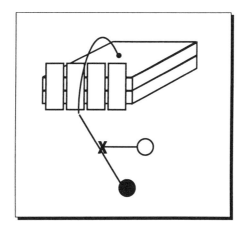

Drill #25: Drive-Through Drill

Objective: To practice maintaining proper drive and follow-through after contact.

Equipment Needed: Two blocking dummies, footballs.

Description: The center, quarterback, and running back set up on the ten yard line, going in. Two defenders with blocking dummies are positioned facing each other on the seven yard line. The quarterback takes the snap and hands off to the running back, who attempts to explode through the bags and continue into the end zone. The defenders attempt to jam the running back with the dummies.

Coaching Points:

- The running back should arch his back, maintain a good foot base, and pump his knees to maintain his balance and continue into the end zone. The coach may signal the defenders to fake the jam and offer no resistance. In this case, if the runner is overextending himself, he will fall forward instead of being able to continue his run.

- The ballcarrier should cover the ball with his free hand and arm just before making contact.

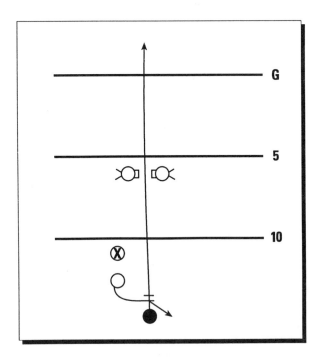

Drill #26: Stumble-Balance Drill

Objective: To teach running backs to regain their balance when stumbling.

Equipment Needed: Footballs.

Description: Running backs take a five-yard running start and then touch the palm of their hand to the next yard line, causing themselves to stumble. They should buck their head, arch their back, stick out their chest, and pump their knees in order to regain their balance. After regaining their balance, the running backs switch the ball to the other arm, run five more yards, and touch the opposite hand to the next yard line. The stumble is repeated four times.

Coaching Point:

- The coach should make sure the ballcarriers touch their palm, not their fingertips, to the ground to cause the stumble.

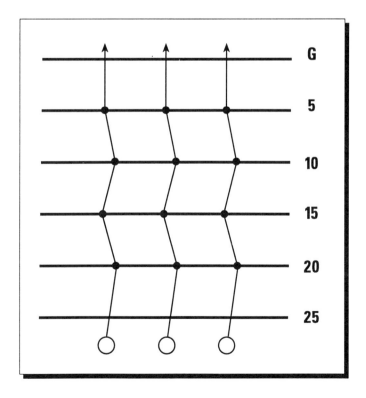

Drill #27: Dead Weight Drill

Objective: To teach running backs to drive ahead while dragging a defender.

Equipment Needed: Footballs.

Description: Half the running backs are given footballs and positioned on the ten yard line. The rest of the backs line up behind the ballcarriers and grasp them around the waist to simulate defenders. The ballcarriers then drive the ten yards to the end zone using body lean, high knee pumping, proper foot base, and good ball security.

Coaching Points:

- The coach should emphasize the proper techniques for driving while dragging a defender.

- The backs acting as defenders should make it as difficult as they can for the ballcarriers to reach the end zone.

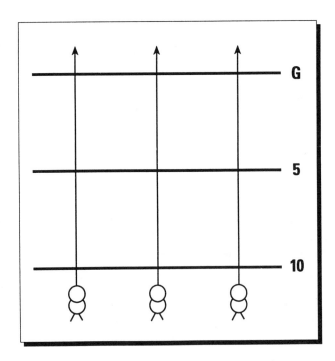

Drill #28: Obstacle Run

Objective: To practice reading, protecting the ball, quickness, reaction, balance, and explosion.

Equipment Needed: Five large barrels, three large blocking dummies, footballs.

Description: Four barrels are positioned at the corners of a two-yard square, with the fifth barrel in the middle. A defender is positioned behind each of the back two barrels. The three dummies are set up in a triangle three yards behind the barrels, with the dummies a yard apart. The coach is positioned behind the middle barrel, and the ballcarriers form a line five yards in front of the square. Each ballcarrier is given a football. The first running back sprints between the first two barrels as the coach appears on either side of the middle barrel. The running back cuts around the middle barrel in the opposite direction. As he passes the last two barrels, the defenders stationed behind them try to dislodge the ball. The ballcarrier then hits the middle dummy and spins left or right, then cuts around the back dummy on that side.

Coaching Points:

- The coach should emphasize using the correct stance and carrying the ball properly.

- Running backs should use a lateral step when cutting away from the coach and keep their heads up throughout the drill.

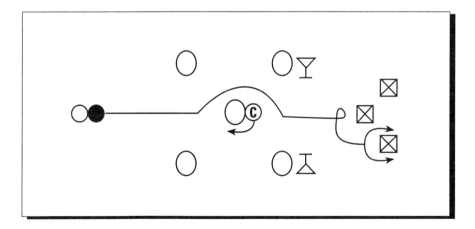

Drill #29: Explosion Drill

Objective: To teach the fundamentals of running the football.

Equipment Needed: Three large blocking dummies, footballs.

Description: Two players with dummies are stationed a yard apart on a designated line of scrimmage. A player with the third dummy is positioned three yards behind the first two. A quarterback is aligned a yard in front of either dummy on the line of scrimmage, with running backs positioned five yards back from the line. On the quarterback's signal, the first running back sprints forward, receives the handoff, and attempts to explode through the two dummies as the defenders try to jam him. He then hits the third dummy, spins to either side, and sprints ten yards downfield.

Coaching Points:

- The coach should instruct the running backs to keep their eyes straight ahead when receiving the handoff.

- Handoffs should be practiced from both sides.

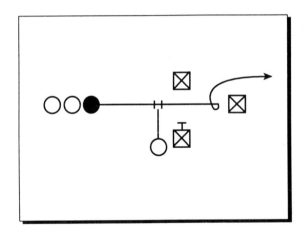

Drill #30: Tunnel Drill

Objective: To practice stances and take-offs.

Equipment Needed: One lineman's chute, footballs.

Description: Off the quarterback's cadence, the backs drive from their stances through the lineman's cute. If desired, the quarterback can hand the ball off to the back as he leaves his stance. The running back should practice straight ahead and angled take-offs.

Coaching Points:

- The coach should check all aspects of the stance and take-off.

- When practicing the angled take-off, the running back's stance should face the opposite back post of the chute.

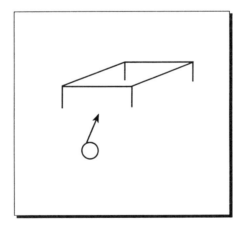

Drill #31: Take Off for the Landmark Drill

Objective: To practice stances and takeoffs.

Equipment Needed: One line spacing tape, footballs.

Description: The coach calls a play and two running backs position themselves properly behind the tape. The coach calls cadence and the backs drive out of their stance and take off for the appropriate landmark.

Coaching Point:

• The coach should check all aspects of the running backs' stance and takeoff and make sure they are aiming for the correct landmark.

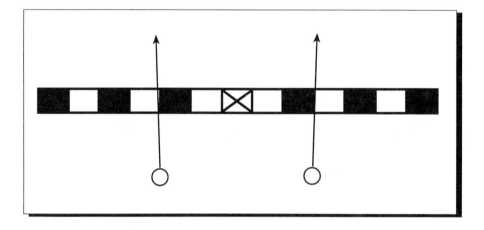

Drill #32: Option Pitch Drill

Objective: To practice receiving the option pitch.

Equipment Needed: One cone, footballs.

Description: A quarterback is positioned on one knee at a 45-degree angle to the desired pitch point, which is marked with a cone. Running backs form a line at an appropriate pre-snap position. On a signal from the quarterback, the first back in line takes off for the pitch point, receiving the pitch from the quarterback just outside the cone.

Coaching Points:

- The coach should emphasize the importance of proper timing to the option pitch.

- The pitch should be practiced to both sides.

- The coach may split the running backs into three or four groups and have each group work with a different quarterback to shorten the amount of time needed to complete the drill.

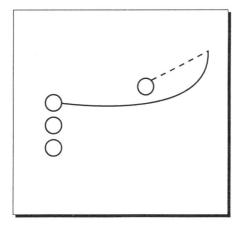

Drill #33: Square Drill

Objective: To develop agility, balance, and body control; to improve footwork.

Equipment Needed: Four rags, footballs.

Description: The four rags are placed at the corners of a ten-yard square, and running backs are positioned in a line ten yards from one corner. On the coach's command, the first running back in line sprints to the first rag and circles it, then continues around the square, repeating the process.

Coaching Points:

- The drill should be performed at full speed.

- The running backs should place their inside hand on the rags as they circle them.

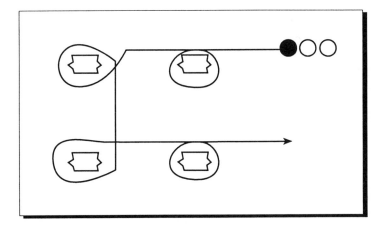

Drill #34: Through the Hole Drill

Objective: To practice cutting off the blocker and exploding through the hole.

Equipment Needed: Two cones, footballs.

Description: An offensive lineman and defensive lineman are positioned opposite each other on a designated line of scrimmage. Cones are placed on either side of the offensive lineman, approximately one yard out. The quarterback hands off to the running back, and the offensive lineman blocks his opponent. The running back takes off after receiving the ball and cuts off the lineman's block, staying between the blocker and the cone.

Coaching Points:

- The running back should practice cutting off handoffs to both sides.

- The running back should be prepared to use a shoulder drive technique if the defender is not blocked effectively.

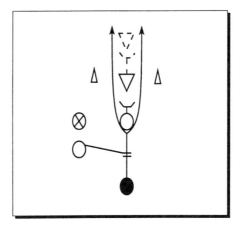

Drill #35: Skeleton Dive Drill

Objective: To practice the dive technique.

Equipment Needed: Footballs.

Description: Three offensive linemen and three defensive linemen are positioned on a designated line of scrimmage. Two or three backs are positioned behind the quarterback. The offense is given three downs to make five yards using the dive technique. The quarterback receives the snap and hands off to the back designated by the coach. If the ballcarrier is one of the outside backs, he dives to either side of the lineman in front of him. If the ballcarrier is the back behind the quarterback, he dives to either side of the center. The coach may also choose to have the quarterback keep the ball. In this case, the quarterback receives the snap and dives to either side of the center.

Coaching Points:

- The coach should check all aspects of the players' dive technique.

- Competition may be fostered by awarding points to the offense for making five yards or to the defense for stopping the offensive drive.

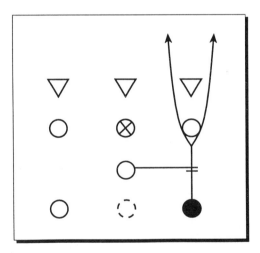

Drill #36: Up the Sideline Drill

Objective: To practice runs up the sideline.

Equipment Needed: Three air dummies, footballs.

Description: Three defenders with air dummies are positioned two or three yards from the sideline. A center and quarterback are positioned two yards back on the near hash mark, with the running back aligned behind the quarterback. The quarterback receives the snap and pitches to the running back, who breaks up the sideline past the defenders, who try to force him out of bounds.

Coaching Points:

- The ballcarrier should secure the ball under his outside arm and use his inside arm to ward off blows.

- Knee pumping and a proper foot base are necessary for the ballcarrier to maintain his balance.

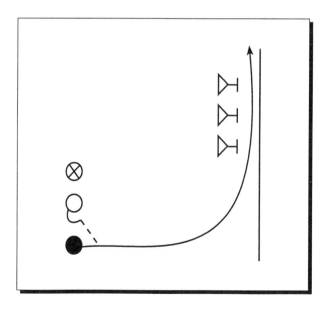

Drill #37: Corner Flag Drill

Objective: To practice the dive squeeze technique; to practice getting into the end zone inside the corner flag.

Equipment Needed: Two large blocking dummies, footballs, an end zone equipped with corner flags.

Description: The two dummies are positioned a yard apart two yards out from the corner flag on a 45-degree angle. They are held by defenders or extra running backs. The center is stationed on the seven yard line, with the quarterback and running back lined up behind him. The quarterback takes the snap and hands off or pitches to the running back, who drives toward the corner, attempting to explode through the dummies and into the end zone. The players holding the dummies attempt to jam the ballcarrier and keep him from reaching the end zone.

Coaching Points:

- The running back should cover the ball with his free hand and arm just before making contact.

- The running back should stay low and aim for a point just inside the flag.

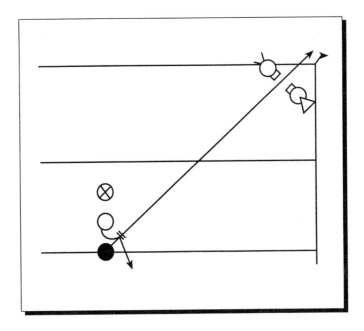

Drill #38: Slippery Handoff Drill

Objective: To teach and practice the fundamentals of receiving and carrying a wet football.

Equipment Needed: Eight large blocking dummies, a bucket of water, footballs.

Description: Two defenders with blocking dummies are positioned a yard apart on a designated line of scrimmage. Three more dummies are laid two yards apart on the ground parallel to the line of scrimmage, with the first dummy one yard behind the defenders. Players are stationed on each end of the three dummies, forming a gauntlet. The last three dummies are positioned in a triangle seven yards behind the last dummy on the ground, with the coach holding the lead dummy of the triangle. The quarterback is positioned on the line of scrimmage, with a running back near him in a specific play alignment. The quarterback wets footballs in a bucket of water and calls cadence. The running back sprints forward, receives the wet football from the quarterback, and blasts through the first two dummies while the defenders try to jam him, and over the next three as the players in the gauntlet try to dislodge the football. As the running back clears the gauntlet, the coach tilts his dummy to one side. The running back cuts the opposite way and sprints between the final dummies.

Coaching Points:

- The drill should be conducted at full speed.

- The coach should emphasize the importance of properly securing the football.

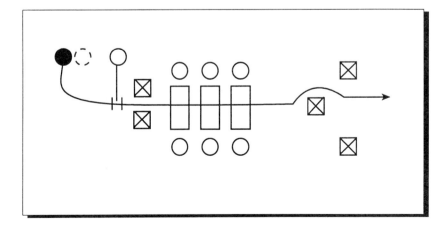

Drill #39: Arm Exchange Drill

Objective: To practice switching the ball from one arm to the other.

Equipment Needed: Footballs.

Description: The running backs are divided into pairs. One back in each pair practices changing the ball from arm to arm using the proper ball change technique. His partner attempts to dislodge the ball by slapping, punching, and grabbing. After a specified amount of time, the backs switch places and repeat the drill.

Coaching Point:

- The coach should check all aspects of the backs' ball change technique.

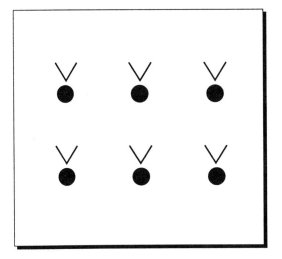

Drill #40: Ball Protection Drill

Objective: To practice protecting the football.

Equipment Needed: Footballs.

Description: The running backs are divided into pairs. One back in each pair is designated as the ballcarrier. The other back is positioned two yards in from of him and slightly to his right. The ballcarrier initially uses a one-armed carry with his right arm. On a signal from the coach, his partner delivers a blow. The ballcarrier should react by executing a two-hand carry and absorbing the blow by covering the ball with his free hand and arm. After four or five blows, the ballcarrier switches the ball to his other arm and his partner takes a position slightly to his left to repeat the drill. The backs then change places and run the drill again.

Coaching Points:

- After each blow, the ballcarrier removes his free hand and arm from the ball, enabling him to practice executing the two-hand carry with each blow.

- The partner may be allowed to add punches, slaps, and rips with each blow in an attempt to dislodge the ball.

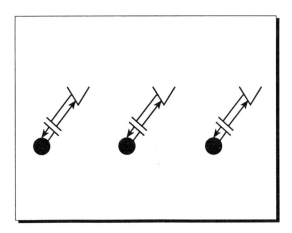

Drill #41: Double Time Ball Protection Drill

Objective: To practice protecting the football.

Equipment Needed: Footballs.

Description: The running backs are divided into groups of three. One back in each group is designated as the ballcarrier. The other two backs are positioned two yards in front of him, one to the right and one to the left. The ballcarrier initially uses a one-armed carry. On a signal from the coach, one of the other backs delivers a blow. The ballcarrier reacts by executing a two-hand carry while the blow is being delivered. He then removes his free hand and receives a blow from the other back. On each blow, the ballcarrier must execute the two-hand carry and protect the football. After a designated time period, the three backs rotate and repeat the drill.

Coaching Point:

• The blows should be close together, but not so close that the ballcarrier does not have a chance to react and perform the two-hand carry.

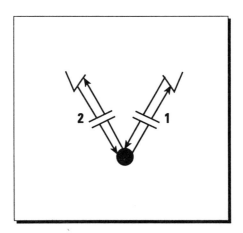

Drill #42: Monkey Roll

Objective: To improve ball security.

Equipment Needed: Footballs.

Description: Running backs are divided into three lines positioned two yards apart on a yard line. The first back in each line has a football. On the coach's command, these three backs step forward five yards. The back in the middle dives and rolls to his right. The back on the right dives sideways over the middle back and rolls left. The back on the left dives over the second back and rolls to his right. At the end of their roll, the backs regain their feet and repeat this process six or seven times.

Coaching Points:

- Running backs should secure the football before diving.

- The drill should be performed at full speed.

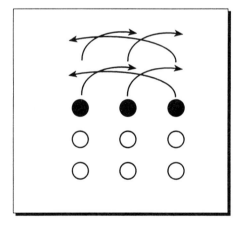

Drill #43: Runner's Gauntlet

Objective: To improve ball security.

Equipment Needed: Hand shields, footballs.

Description: Two rows of players are positioned facing each other, leaving an open lane between them 1.5 yards wide. The players in the rows are all one yard apart. A line of ballcarriers in positioned five yards back from the opening of the lane. Ballcarriers run the gauntlet as quickly and powerfully as possible while protecting the ball. The players in the gauntlet punch, slap, grab, and use hand shields to jam the ballcarrier and dislodge the ball.

Coaching Points:

- The coach may add a center and quarterback to the drill and require running backs to receive the ball from the handoff.

- The coach should emphasize arching the back, pumping the knees, and protecting the ball.

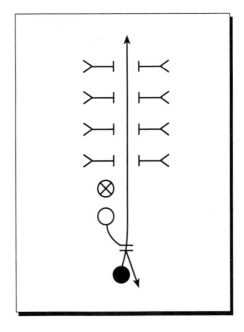

CHAPTER 3

END DRILLS

Drill #44: Cutting Drill

Objective: To improve players' cutting ability.

Equipment Needed: Four cones, footballs.

Description: Four cones are placed at the corners of a ten-yard square. Players maneuver around the cones in a "bow tie" shape, making two 45-degree cuts off each foot.

Coaching Point:

- Players should begin this drill at a slow pace and increase their speed as their proficiency improves.

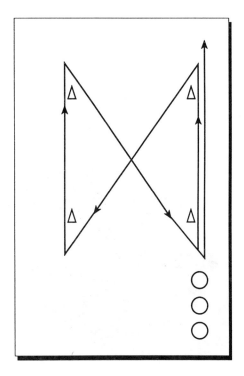

Drill #45: Catching Drill

Objective: To improve players' catching ability.

Equipment Needed: Footballs.

Description: The ends are divided into pairs. Players face each other at a distance of five yards and throw the ball sharply back and forth, aiming at the numbers, over the head, and at either knee.

Coaching Point:

• Players should focus on keeping their eyes on the ball.

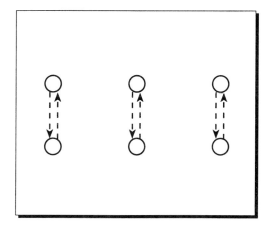

Drill #46: Fly Drill

Objective: To improve players' catching ability.

Equipment Needed: Footballs.

Description: Two quarterbacks are positioned on opposite hash marks 30 yards apart. The ends split into two groups, each forming a line to a quarterback's right. On a signal from the quarterback, the first end in line runs downfield. The quarterback throws the ball over the end's outside shoulder with a trajectory that allows him to adjust to the ball. After making the catch, the receiver continues downfield, gives the ball to the other quarterback, and goes to the end of that line.

Coaching Points:

- The coach should emphasize proper reception technique.

- This drill allows quarterbacks to practice throwing the over-the-shoulder pass.

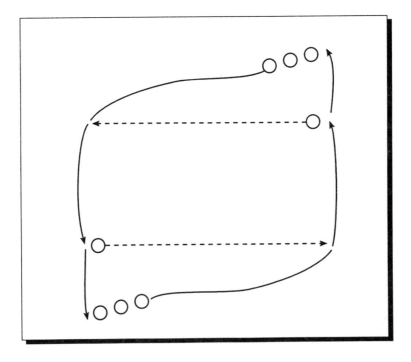

Drill #47: Bad Ball Drill

Objective: To improve players' catching ability.

Equipment Needed: Footballs.

Description: The ends form a line along a designated yard line. The coach positions himself 10 yards away. One at a time, the ends run down the line and dive to catch balls thrown low and away by the coach, then roll.

Coaching Point:

• Players should get their hands under the ball and cradle it into their body as they roll.

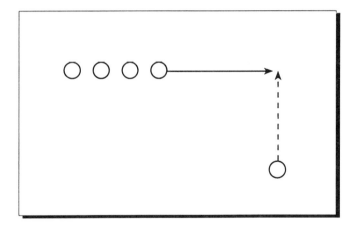

Drill #48: Receiver Gauntlet

Objective: To improve players' catching and ball protection skills.

Equipment Needed: Footballs.

Description: Six to eight players form a gauntlet upfield from a designated line of scrimmage. The end runs a 45-degree pattern and catches the ball over his outside shoulder, then tucks the ball away, turns upfield, and runs through the gauntlet as the other players try to dislodge the ball.

Coaching Points:

- Players should concentrate on catching the ball before making their turn upfield.

- Players should have the ball secured before entering the gauntlet.

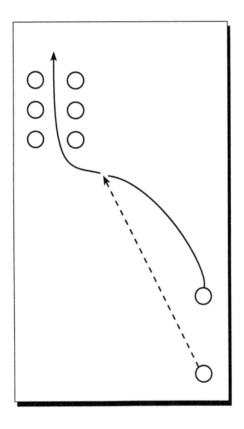

Drill #49: Sideline Drill

Objective: To improve players' ability to catch the ball and remain inbounds.

Equipment Needed: Footballs.

Description: Receivers line up five yards inside the sideline. The first player in line releases with width, making his cut at eight yards. The coach throws the ball at the sideline, forcing the receiver to concentrate on catching the ball with one foot inbounds.

Coaching Point:

• Players should focus on being aware of their position in relation to the sideline before they attempt to make the catch.

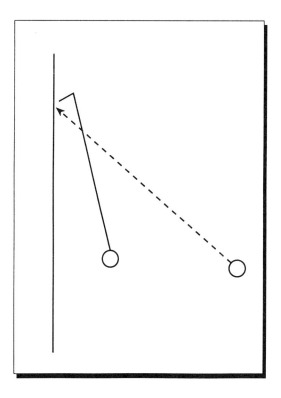

Drill #50: Clock Drill

Objective: To improve players' catching abilities.

Equipment Needed: Footballs.

Description: The ends are split into pairs. Partners face each other at a distance of five yards and throw the ball sharply back and forth. Players should work around their partner's body, aiming for where the numbers would be on a clock.

Coaching Point:

- The coach should emphasize good reception techniques.

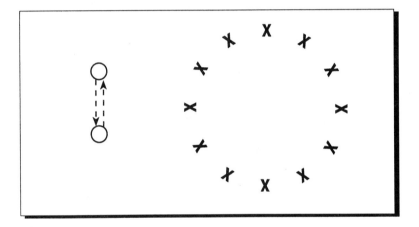

Drill #51: Side Run High

Objective: To improve players' catching abilities.

Equipment Needed: Footballs.

Description: The ends form a line along a designated yard line. The first player in line begins running along the yard line across the field. The coach throws a pass over the end's head. The end should jump to catch the ball and continue across the field without stopping.

Coaching Points:

- The coach's pass should be high enough that the receiver must jump to catch it for this drill to be effective.

- The coach should emphasize proper reception techniques.

- This drill should be conducted running to both the left and the right.

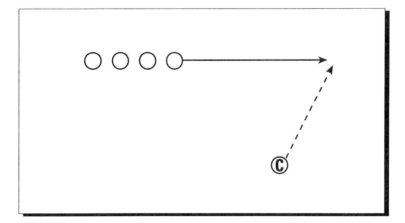

Drill #52: Side Run Low

Objective: To improve players' catching abilities.

Equipment Needed: Footballs.

Description: The ends form a line on a designated yard line. The first player in line begins running across the field along the yard line. The coach throws a low pass, and the receiver should bend over to catch the ball and continue across the field without stopping.

Coaching Points:

- The coach should emphasize proper reception techniques.

- The drill should be conducted running to both the left and the right.

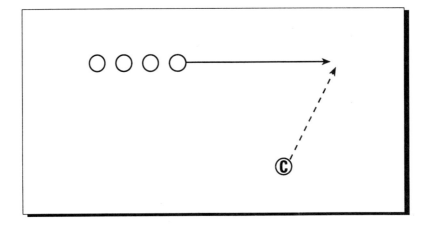

Drill #53: Side Run Behind

Objective: To improve players' catching abilities.

Equipment Needed: Footballs.

Description: The ends form a line on a designated yard line. The first player in line begins running along the yard line across the field. The coach throws a pass behind the player. The receiver should turn his head and reach back to catch the ball, then continue across the field without stopping.

Coaching Points:

- The coach should make sure players do not slow down in an effort to keep the pass from arriving behind them.

- The coach should emphasize good reception techniques.

- The drill should be conducted running to both the left and the right.

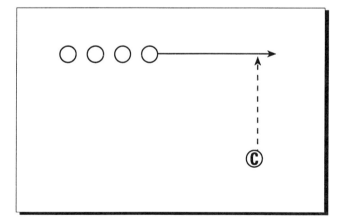

Drill #54: Over Shoulder In Front

Objective: To improve players' catching abilities.

Equipment Needed: Footballs.

Description: The ends should be divided into pairs. One player jogs in place with his back to his partner and his head turned to one side. The partner throws high, medium, and low passes to the side to which the receiver's head is turned. After a designated number of passes, the receiver turns his head to the other side and the drill is repeated. The players then switch places and the drill continues.

Coaching Points:

- The coach should emphasize good reception techniques.

- Players should keep their eyes on the ball until it is securely in their hands.

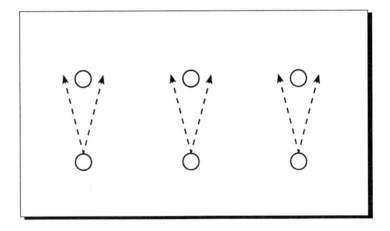

Drill #55: Over Shoulder Behind

Objective: To improve players' catching abilities.

Equipment Needed: Footballs.

Description: The ends are divided into pairs. One player jogs in place with his back to his partner. His head is turned to one side, and his partner throws high, medium, and low passes to the opposite side. The receiver turns his head and shoulders, finds the ball, and makes the catch. After a designated number of passes, the receiver turns his head to the other side and the drill is repeated. The players then switch roles and the drill continues.

Coaching Points:

• The coach should emphasize good reception techniques.

• The receiver should whip his head and shoulders around to find the ball and make the catch.

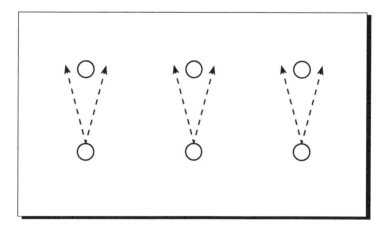

Drill #56: Over Shoulder High

Objective: To improve players' catching abilities.

Equipment Needed: Footballs.

Description: The ends should be divided into pairs. One players jogs in place with his back to his partner and his head turned to either side. His partner throws passes over his head, and the receiver should either jump to catch them or run under them to make the catch. After a designated number of passes, the players switch places and repeat the drill.

Coaching Points:

- The coach should emphasize good reception techniques.

- The passes should be high enough that players can not simply stretch their arms up to catch the ball.

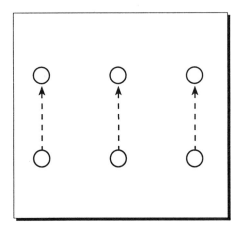

Drill #57: Come Back High

Objective: To improve players' catching abilities.

Equipment Needed: Footballs.

Description: The ends are divided into pairs. One player runs four yards, stutter steps or plants, and comes straight back toward his partner. The partner throws high passes that the receiver must jump to catch. After a specified number of passes, the players switch places and repeat the drill.

Coaching Points:

- The passes should be thrown high enough that the receiver must jump to make the catch.

- The coach should emphasize good reception techniques.

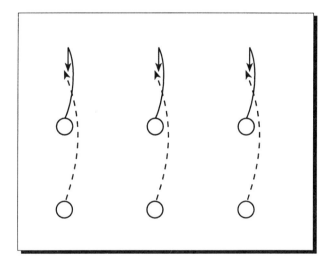

Drill #58: Come Back Low

Objective: To improve players' catching abilities.

Equipment Needed: Footballs.

Description: The ends should be divided into pairs. One player runs four yards, stutter steps or plants, and comes straight back toward his partner. The partner throws low passes that the receiver must bend down to catch.

Coaching Point:

- The coach should emphasize good reception techniques.

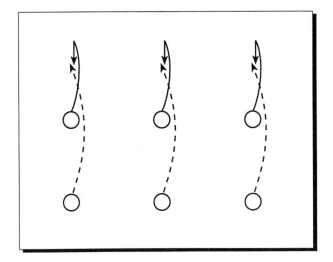

Drill #59: Distraction Drill

Objective: To improve players' ability to catch the ball in distracting conditions.

Equipment Needed: Footballs.

Description: The ends are divided into two groups: defenders and receivers. The defenders are positioned on a designated yard line. The receivers form a line perpendicular to the selected yard line, with the first receiver taking a position two yards in front of the first defender. The coach, stationed fifteen yards behind the defenders, throws a pass to the first receiver, while the defender attempts to distract the receiver by grabbing, pushing, or pulling him or waving his arms in front of him. After the pass is caught or falls incomplete, the defender and receiver go to the end of the opposite line.

Coaching Point:

• The coach should emphasize concentration; receivers should watch the ball until it is securely in their hands.

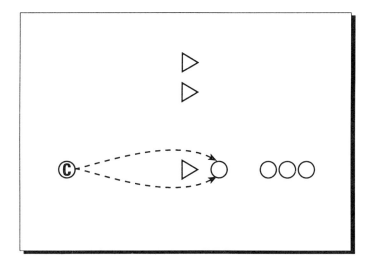

Drill #60: Poor Pass Drill

Objective: To improve players' ability to catch a poorly thrown pass.

Equipment Needed: Footballs.

Description: Ends form a straight line behind a designated line of scrimmage. On the coach's signal, the first player in line runs downfield at three-quarter speed, looking for a pass over his inside shoulder. The coach makes a poorly thrown pass to the receiver's outside shoulder, forcing him to adjust and make the catch.

Coaching Point:

- When turning to make the catch, the ends should whip their head and shoulders around to the outside.

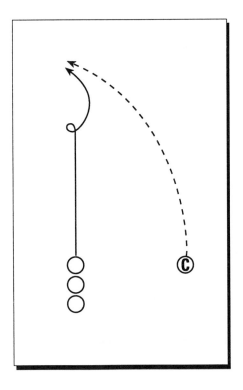

Drill #61: Spin Catch Drill

Objective: To develop players' catching reactions.

Equipment Needed: Footballs.

Description: One end is positioned with his back to the coach at a distance of about 12 yards. The other ends form a line off to the side. The coach throws a hard pass to some point around the receiver downfield. When the ball has traveled about a yard, the players in line yell "Ball," signaling the receiver to spin around, find the ball, and make the catch.

Coaching Points:

- The coach should vary the location of his throws to make the receiver's job more difficult.

- The players in line should not signal the receiver too early.

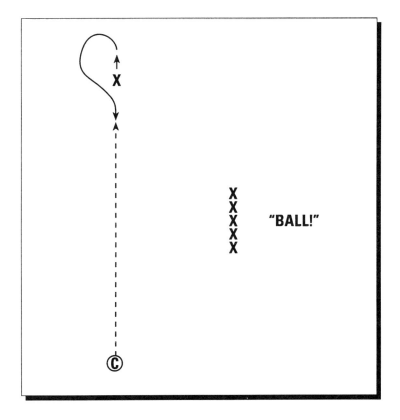

Drill #62: On the Run Drill

Objective: To practice catching the ball on the run.

Equipment Needed: Footballs.

Description: The ends form a line even with the coach. The first player in line runs a designated pattern. The coach throws the ball so the receiver will have to adjust to the ball and catch it on the move, continuing his designated route.

Coaching Points:

- The coach should vary the timing and location of his throws.

- Patterns should be run to both the left and the right.

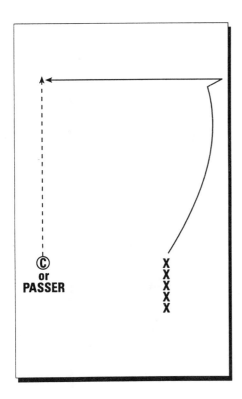 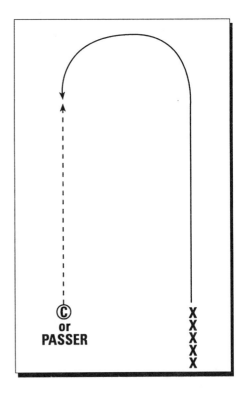

Drill #63: Tip Drill

Objective: To teach the fundamentals of catching a pass.

Equipment Needed: Footballs.

Description: Ends are divided into pairs and placed on yard lines five yards apart. They should begin on one sideline. The coach throws a soft pass to one of the two ends. The two players tip the ball back and forth as they run the width of the field, alternating hands after each tip.

Coaching Points:

- The players should watch the flight of the football at all times.

- Each pair of players should try to tip the ball at least 10 times before reaching the opposite sideline.

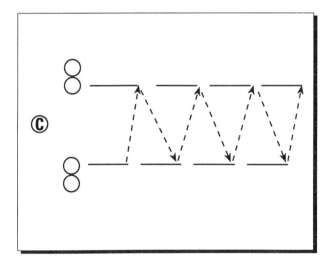

Drill #64: Numbered Ball Drill

Objective: To improve players' concentration when catching the football.

Equipment Needed: Footballs with one-inch numbers painted on each panel, three hand shields.

Description: Three players are given hand shields and positioned in a triangle, three yards apart. Ends form a line to the right of the triangle. The first end in line runs to the center of the triangle, receives a pass, and calls out the number on the football as the other players jam him with their shields. After a specified number of rotations, the ends move to the left side of the triangle.

Coaching Points:

- Players should watch the ball until it is securely in their hands.

- Coaches should make sure players call out the correct number after making the catch.

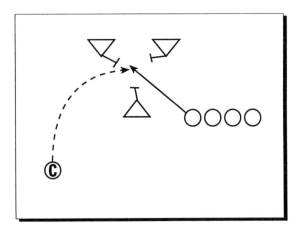

Drill #65: Crush Drill

Objective: To develop concentration; to develop a player's ability to catch and hang onto the ball in a crowd.

Equipment Needed: Four air dummies.

Description: Four players with air dummies are positioned in the reception area of a pass route. The ends runs the chosen route, and the coach passes the ball. While the ball is in the air, the players with dummies try to distract the receiver by waving their hands and the dummies or running in front of him. When the end makes the catch, the other players try to knock the ball loose using their hands or the air dummies.

Coaching Points:

• The coach should vary the exact timing and location of his throws.

• The coach should emphasize concentration and proper ball security techniques.

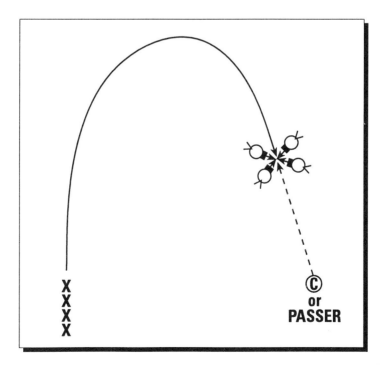

Drill #66: Obstruction Drill

Objective: To teach players to catch the ball in spite of obstacles on the ground.

Equipment Needed: Three blocking dummies.

Description: The dummies are placed in a line, about four feet apart. The end runs a route which takes him over the bags. As he is hopping over the bags, the coach passes the ball and the end must make the catch.

Coaching Point:

• The coach should vary the timing and location of the passes to create different scenarios for the players.

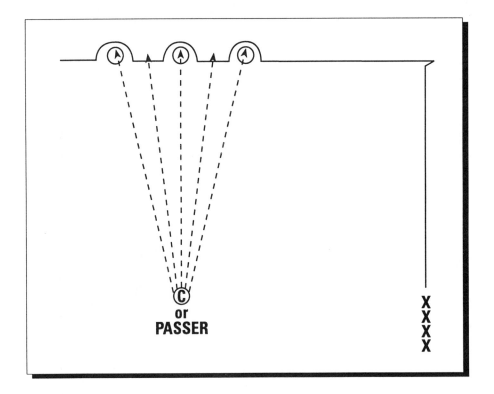

Drill #67: End Release Drill

Objective: To teach the fundamentals of inside and outside line releases.

Equipment Needed: One large blocking dummy, one hand shield.

Description: A tight end is positioned on a designated line of scrimmage with a defender over his outside shoulder holding a hand shield. The dummy is laid in the neutral zone at the tackle position. The coach calls cadence and the tight end releases off the line while the defender tries to jam him. He uses a swim or lower shoulder drive technique and switches between inside and outside releases.

Coaching Points:

- Tight ends should be in their proper stances.

- The coach should check all aspects of the end's release technique.

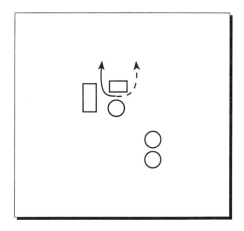

Drill #68: Open Tight End Drill

Objective: To teach the techniques used to get open in the underneath hash area.

Equipment Needed: Three large blocking dummies, footballs.

Description: A quarterback is positioned on the right hash mark of a designated line of scrimmage. The ends form two lines, one five yards to the left of the quarterback and one five yards to the right. Players holding the dummies are positioned twelve yards downfield, one in front of the quarterback and one in front of each line of ends. On the quarterback's cadence, the designated tight end releases downfield and works for position between the middle dummy and the dummy to his side. If the quarterback holds the ball, the end works to get open on the other side. After the cadence, the quarterback takes a specific drop and finds the end between either pair of dummies. After making the catch, the end returns to the opposite line.

Coaching Point:

- Tight ends should be in their proper stances and execute their release techniques correctly.

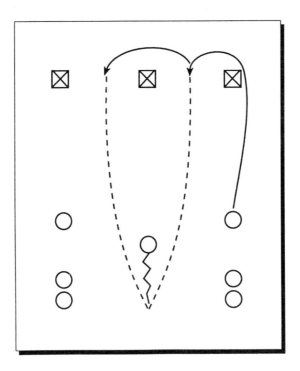

CHAPTER 4

OFFENSIVE LINE DRILLS

Drill #69: Waggle Guard Drill

Objective: To isolate the guard pulling and reading technique needed for the Waggle.

Equipment Needed: Five cones and two small hand-shields.

Description: The guards practice the appropriate technique for pulling on the Waggle. The lead guard executes a log pull and the backside guard executes a long sweep pull. The coach may evolve the basic drill to a read drill by having shield number one charge upfield on a defensive stunt forcing the lead guard to kick the shield out. The backside guard must read the action of the lead guard. If the lead guard logs, the backside guard kicks out shield number two. If the lead guard kicks out, the backside guard can log at the edge. The coach may still increase the difficulty of the drill by directing the shield holders to run an X stunt, forcing the lead guard to kick out as the backside guard logs.

Coaching Points:

- The coach should stand in front of the drill to check the focus of the guard's eyes.

- The coach emphasizes that the Waggle will be likely be set up for a situation in which shield number one will be logged and shield number two will be kicked out.

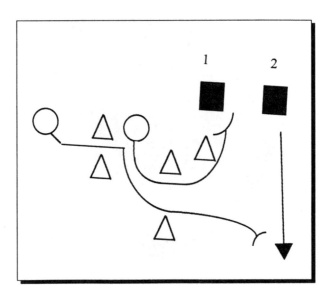

Drill #70: Buck Sweep Guard Drill

Objective: To develop the guard's hammer pull and wall pull on the buck sweep.

Equipment Needed: Two large dummies, two small hand shields, and five cones.

Description: Two guard lines are formed. The large dummies are laid on the ground as shown. One shield holder stands at position 1 and another shield holder stands at position 2. The lead guards pulls to a 3 yard depth and hammer blocks through the large dummies. The backside guard pulls on the inside hip of the hammer guard and drives through shield number one. The backside guard uses his inside shoulder to deliver a blow on the shield as he continues downfield for 10 yards. The drill is flipped over for the buck sweep to the left.

Coaching Point:

- The coach checks to see if the guards enter the alley with their shoulders square.

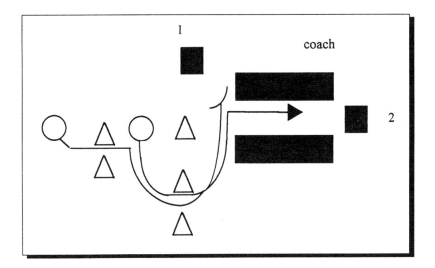

Drill #71: Short Trap Drill

Objective: To teach the lead post and inside-out (trap) blocks.

Equipment Needed: Two large blocking dummies.

Description: A center and two guards are positioned on a designated line of scrimmage. One dummy is placed over the center, the other over the tackle position. On the coach's signal, the center and frontside guard lead post block the dummy on the center and the backside guard pulls across the center and traps the dummy over the tackle. The backside guard takes a short step with his inside foot, then adjusts tight to the lead post on his second step, which gets his head upfield and puts him in a good position to trap.

Coaching Point:

* The coach should check players' blocking techniques.

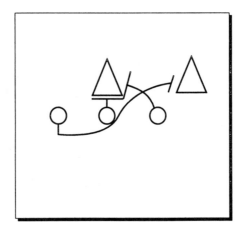

Drill #72: Gut Drill

Objective: To teach a lineman to pull through the hole to block a linebacker.

Equipment Needed: Three large blocking dummies.

Description: A center and two guards are positioned on a designated line of scrimmage. One dummy is positioned as a linebacker over the center; the others are positioned over the guards. On the coach's signal, the frontside guard pulls away to act as a false key. The center blocks back on the dummy over the backside guard. The backside guard pulls behind the center with a short step, then stays low and tight to the center and turns up through the hole to block the linebacker, placing his head to the attack side.

Coaching Point:

• The coach should emphasize good blocking technique.

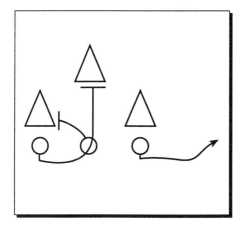

Drill #73: Shoulder Block Blow Delivery Drill

Objective: To practice upper body technique of a shoulder block.

Equipment Needed: Hand-held shields.

Description: Players align in front of the available shield holders. The shield holders crouch so that the shield is held at knee level. The blocker pushes off his left foot and steps with his right foot. The following step of the push foot drives the inside shoulder to the face of the shield. The shoulder lifts the shield. The blocker should knock the shield holder backward. The blocker should land on his belt buckle and execute a seat roll to the side of the shoulder block.

Coaching Points:

- Proper hip extension will result in the blocker's upper body hitting the ground in progression from belt buckle to shoulders.

- The shield must be hit at an upward angle and the shield holder must be knocked backward.

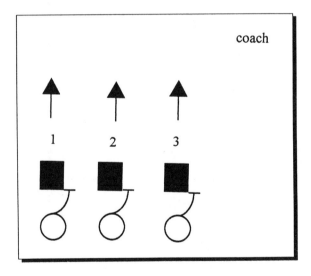

Drill #74: Mixed Scheme Drill

Objective: To teach the fundamentals and techniques of various blocking schemes.

Equipment Needed: Footballs.

Description: An offensive team is aligned on a designated line of scrimmage, with defensive linemen and linebackers positioned opposite them. The coach should stand behind the offense to observe the drill. The offensive team huddles and then runs five different plays in quick succession (no huddle is allowed between plays) while the defense reacts to the blocks and pursues the ballcarrier.

Coaching Points:

- The offensive team's emphasis should be on executing the blocking schemes correctly.

- The coach may signal the defense to change its alignment at any time.

- The coach should pay special attention to the offensive players' alignments and blocking techniques.

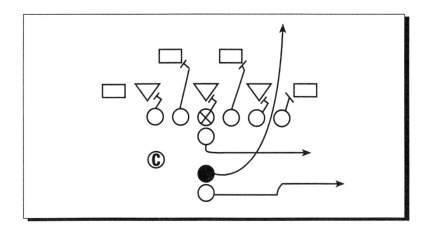

Drill #75: Seven-Man Cutoff Drill

Objective: To practice the cutoff block.

Equipment Needed: A seven-man blocking sled.

Description: Linemen are positioned in front of the sled with their shoulder on the inside of the pad. On the coach's command, they execute a cutoff block. After a designated number of repetitions, the linemen switch to the outside of the pad and repeat the drill.

Coaching Point:

- The coach should check the players' feet, head and shoulders, and forearm blow.

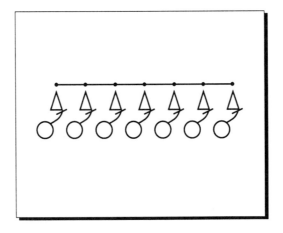

Drill #76 Cutoff and Alley Break Drill

Objective: To perfect the cutoff block and practice the horizontal break to the alley.

Equipment Needed: One large dummy, two small hand-shields, and four cones.

Description: The blocker dips under the large dummy, throwing his outside arm into the large dummy. The blocker continues on an arc inside of the shield-holder at four yards depth. The blocker angles to the cone at a seven yard depth and cuts across the field on a 90 degree angle. The blocker delivers a face-up blow to the second hand-shield. The second hand-shield simulates a linebacker and the third hand-shield simulates a free safety attempting to fill the alley. The coach may alter the drill by having the second shield holder attack the alley from a free safety position to simulate the free safety. In this case, the blocker must get his head across the front of the shield-holder.

Coaching Points:

- The coach should emphasize to the blocker that he must throw an uppercut punch through the large dummy and the simulated linebacker.

- The coach should encourage the blocker to sprint full speed to the alley.

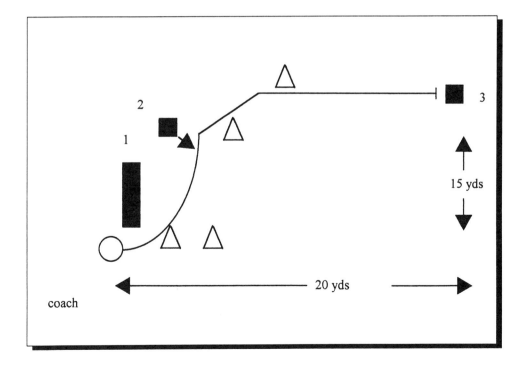

Drill #77: Off the Ball Drill

Objective: To practice the punch and lift of the area block.

Equipment Needed: Two large blocking dummies.

Description: Two lines are formed. Each player area blocks the dummy with the face in the middle of the dummy. The player throws his hands on the snap and punches and lifts the dummy as his feet churn and his hips sink. The players alternate using a right and left push foot.

Coaching Points:

- The blocker should drive the dummy with a lifting motion. The punch of the hands prevents the face from making a forceful contact with the dummy.

- The coach should check the stride length of the first step in order to reinforce the push foot technique.

- Players should block the dummy for a random distance until the whistle is blown. Players should not block for a designated distance.

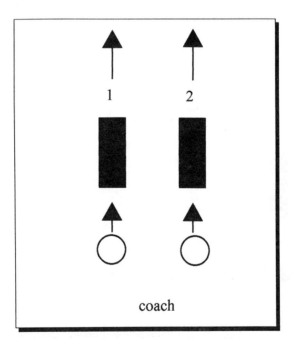

Drill #78: Stick to the Shield Drill

Objective: To teach players to drive off the line of scrimmage and sustain a shoulder block.

Equipment Needed: Four hand shields.

Description: Four offensive linemen are positioned five yards apart on a designate line of scrimmage. A player holding a hand shield is stationed six inches in front of each lineman. In the first phase of the drill, the linemen drive off the line into a layout position on the shield. After a specified number of repetitions, the drill switches to the second phase. In this phase, the linemen begin in their layout position on the shields. On the coach's whistle, the shield holders retreat slowly, changing direction, and the linemen drive their feet and maintain contact with the shield.

Coaching Point:

• The coach should emphasize good blocking techniques.

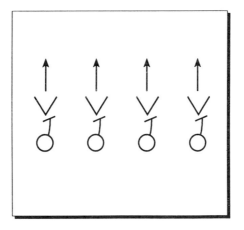

Drill #79: Pass Protection Drill

Objective: To practice pass protection.

Equipment Needed: One large blocking dummy.

Description: The dummy is positioned behind a line of three blockers to represent the quarterback. The blockers are all five yards apart, with a rusher directly across from the first blocker in the line. On the coach's signal, the rusher attempts to reach the "quarterback" any way he can. The blockers use their pass protection techniques to stop the rush.

Coaching Points:

- The coach should emphasize proper blocking techniques.

- The coach may make this a competitive drill by awarding points to the rusher for reaching the quarterback or to the blockers for stopping the rush.

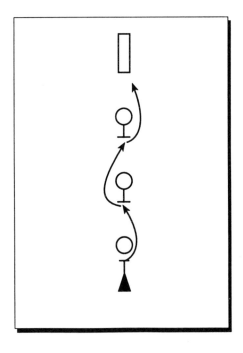

Drill #80: Anchor Sled Attack Drill

Objective: To reinforce the physical nature of attacking a defender.

Equipment Needed: Five man sled anchored by metal stakes.

Description: The linemen are positioned all facing the sled from a position of five yards from the sled. The linemen attack the sled with the left shoulder on command and backpedal to the next pad. The sled is lifted up by the simultaneous contact of the linemen. The linemen quickly back off the sled. The coach may develop the drill to a noncommand drill. If given no command, the linemen learn to work down the sled rhythmically so that the linemen contact the sled in unison. The direction of the linemen is switched and the drill is repeated.

Coaching Points:

• The linemen quickly move off the sled at the highest point of the sled's lift.

• The coach stands behind the sled to ensure that the linemen have their heads up at the moment of contact.

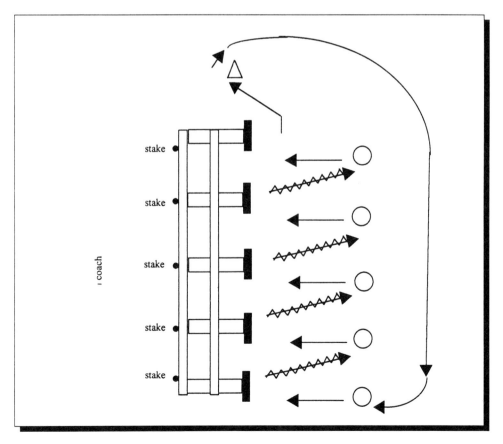

Drill #81: Fire Block Drill

Objective: To teach the technique of the fire block.

Equipment Needed: One large blocking dummy and one hand-held small shield.

Description: The dummy is positioned on the inside shade of the outside blocker. The outside blocker pushes off his inside foot and takes an upfield step at slightly less than 45 degrees. The outside blocker drives his inside shoulder through the outside half of the dummy. The outside blocker uses his inside shoulder to knock the dummy inside to his teammate. The outside blocker continues to the second level and executes an inside shoulder block on the shield-holder. The inside blocker steps laterally with the toe pointed upfield. The trail blocker attempts to get his inside earhole to the hip of the outside blocker. The trail blocker sweeps upfield and places his head across the large dummy. The trail blocker drives the large dummy on a vertical path as he swings his tail around to the inside.

Coaching Points:

- The coach checks for spacing between the blockers. There should be no spacing between the blockers as the trail blocker takes over the large dummy.

- A vertical push on the large dummy should be accomplished before the outside blocker moves to the next level.

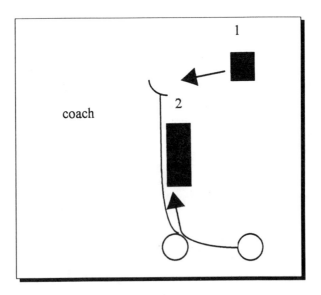

Drill #82: Pull, Trap, and Drive Drill

Objective: To practice pulling, trapping, and driving.

Equipment Needed: One line spacing tape, one large blocking dummy.

Description: The blocker is positioned even with the back edge of the tape. A defender holding the dummy is stationed in the middle of the tape. On the coach's cadence, the blocker pulls along the tape, trap blocks the dummy, and then drives through him.

Coaching Points:

- The coach should emphasize good pulling, trapping, and driving techniques.

- The drill should be run to both the left and the right.

- The defender holding the dummy should increase his pressure as the drill progresses.

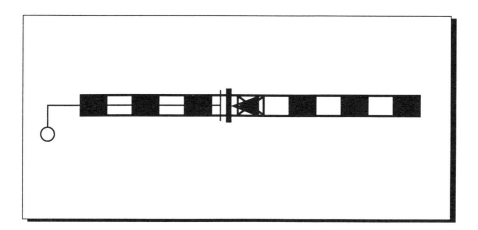

Drill #83: Stick With It Drill

Objective: To practice maintaining contact with a defender after the initial block.

Equipment Needed: One two-man blocking sled.

Description: The offensive linemen form a line in front of one pad on a two-man blocking sled, while the coach stands near the other pad. On the coach's command, the first lineman fires out and executes a shoulder block on the sled. The coach then turns the sled and the lineman works to maintain contact with the pad while the sled is moving.

Coaching Points:

- The coach should check players' stances and blocking techniques.

- Linemen should execute both right and left shoulder blocks.

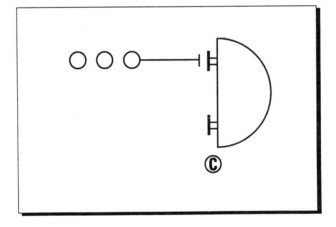

CHAPTER 5

AGILITY AND SPEED DRILLS

Drill #84: Log Drill

Objective: To sharpen the timing of the tackle down block and guard log technique.

Equipment Needed: One large dummy and a small hand-shield.

Description: The tackle blocks down on the large dummy. The large dummy holder alternates between charging across the line and squeezing across the face of the tackle. The guard bucket pulls and logs the hand-shield holder with his inside shoulder. The hand-shield holder closes inside with the tackle's down block.

Coaching Points:

- The coach checks the tackle's footwork to see if he pushes off the opposite foot.

- The tackle places his head across the face of the dummy.

- The coach checks the pulling guard to make sure he is using the correct shoulder to hit the dummy.

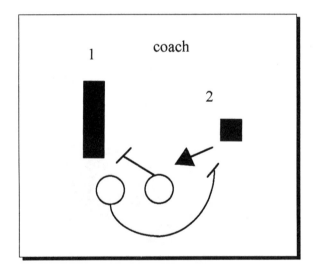

Drill #85: Gap Block Drill

Objective: To practice the angle block technique versus a gap charging defender.

Equipment Needed: Two large dummies and a hand-held small shield.

Description: Two dummies are placed on the ground five to six feet apart. The hand shield holder aligns on the shade of the blocker. On a snap count, the defender charges across the line of scrimmage. The blocker angle blocks the shield holder, using the proper angle block technique.
The coach may widen the shield holder once the blocker becomes skilled at the angle block.
The drill may be run live without the shield.

Coaching Points:

- The blocker must place his head across the defender at the appropriate landmark.

- The blocker must punch the offside arm to the armpit of the gap charging defender.

- The coach should make sure the blocker's head is up.

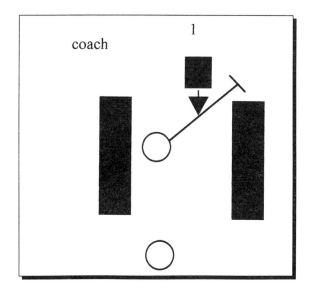

Drill #86: Lead Blocker Drill

Objective: To develop the technique of the double team lead blocker.

Equipment Needed: One large dummy

Description: Two lines are formed three to four feet apart. Players perform the drill in pairs. The players push off the outside foot and use a 45-degree glide step inside. The glide step brings the hips together as the linemen punch the dummy with their inside shoulder and hands. The dummy is driven upfield until the whistle blows.

Coaching Points:

- The player's inside hip must contact his teammate.

- The outside arm must remain free.

- Contact with the dummy should be simultaneous.

- The coach may move around to check to see if the eyes of the blockers are up. The blockers must keep their necks bowed and their eyes up.

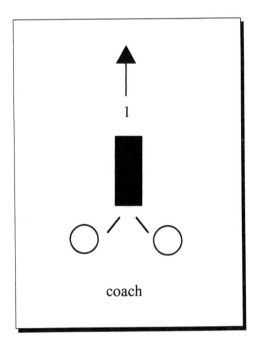

Drill #87: Fullback Belly Drill

Objective: To teach the fullback to keep his shoulders square to the line of scrimmage on the belly.

Equipment Needed: Football, three cones, a large barrel, and one large dummy.

Description: The center snaps the ball and blocks the large dummy for five yards. The fullback runs the belly path and hits the path with his shoulders square. The fullback keeps his eyes up and cuts opposite the coach's movement behind the barrel. The fullback doesn't make the cut before passing the line of scrimmage. The quarterback comes off the ride and runs inside the cone at position number two.

Coaching Points:

- The coach checks to see if the quarterback pulls his hands back to his hip to fake.

- The coach makes the movement after the fullback takes the handoff.

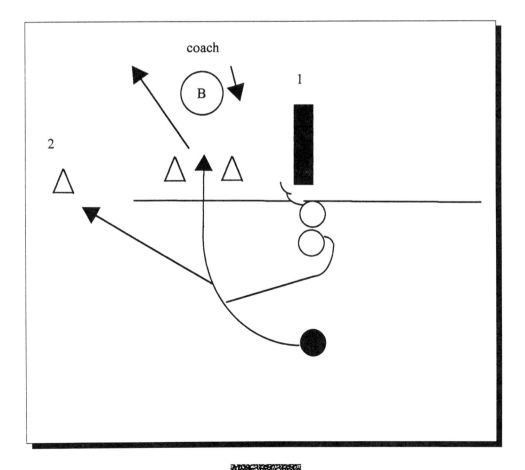

Drill #88: Sally Run Side Drill vs. 4-3 Slide

Objective: To incorporate the guard and center blocking with the quarterback and ball carrier on the Sally play.

Equipment Needed: Football, four cones, two small hand-shields, and one large dummy.

Description: The run blocking side guard and the center perform their appropriate Sally block techniques for a Sally play to the right. The quarterback takes the snap and executes his proper technique on the Sally play. The ball carrier executes his proper technique from the wingback position. The backup quarterback stands at the designated position and flashes a number to the quarterback. The quarterback is required to determine the number after handing off to the ball carrier. The coach may vary the defense to which the Sally is run. The drill is flipped for the Sally play to the left.

Coaching Points:

- The coach checks to see if the ball carrier hits the line of scrimmage with his shoulders square.

- The coach checks to see if the center attacks the large dummy with an aggressive pass protection technique.

- The coach checks to see if the guard makes a 6 inch lateral step on the snap.

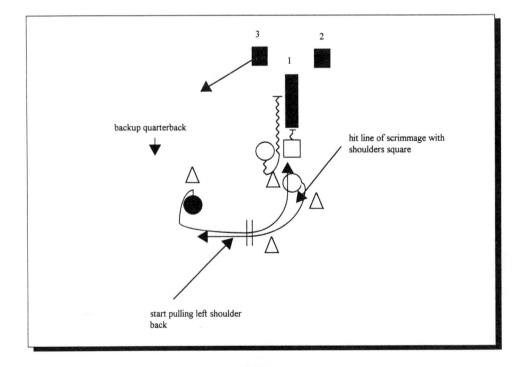

Drill #89: Sally Run Side Drill with Stunt

Objective: To incorporate the guard and center blocking with the quarterback and ball carrier on the Sally play.

Equipment Needed: Football, four cones, two small hand-shields, and one large dummy.

Description: The run blocking side guard and the center perform their appropriate Sally block techniques for a Sally play to the right. The quarterback takes the snap and executes his proper technique on the Sally play. The ball carrier executes his proper technique from the wingback position. The backup quarterback stands at the designated position and flashes a number to the quarterback. The quarterback is required to determine the number after handing off to the ball carrier. The coach may vary the defense to which the Sally is run. The drill is flipped for the Sally play to the left.

Coaching Points:

- The coach checks to see if the ball carrier hits the line of scrimmage with his shoulders square.

- The coach checks to see if the center attacks the large dummy with an aggressive pass protection technique and wheels his tail inside on the stunt.

- The coach checks to see if the guard makes a 6 inch lateral step on the snap.

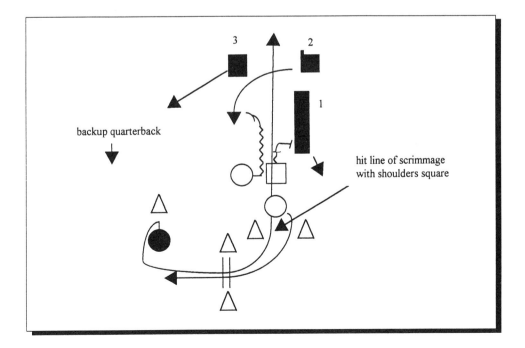

Drill #90: Sally Run Side Drill with Stunt

Objective: To incorporate the guard and center blocking with the quarterback and ball carrier on the Sally play.

Equipment Needed: Football, four cones, two small hand-shields, and one large dummy.

Description: The run blocking side guard and the center perform their appropriate Sally block techniques for a Sally play to the right. The quarterback takes the snap and executes his proper technique on the Sally play. The ball carrier executes his proper technique from the wingback position. The backup quarterback stands at the designated position and flashes a number to the quarterback. The quarterback is required to determine the number after handing off to the ball carrier. The coach may vary the defense to which the Sally is run. The drill is flipped for the Sally play to the left.

Coaching Points:

- The coach checks to see if the ball carrier hits the line of scrimmage with his shoulders square.

- The coach checks to see if the center attacks the large dummy with an aggressive pass protection technique and passes the weak stunting nose to the guard.

- The coach checks to see if the guard makes a 6 inch lateral step on the snap and takes over the nose man in the "A" gap.

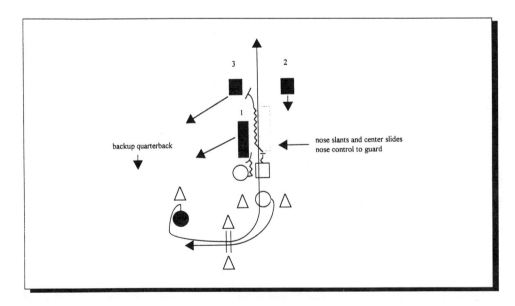

Drill #91: Post-Lead Blocker Read Drill

Objective: To combine the technique of the post block and the lead block of a double team combination versus the two types of defenders, the anchor and stunt defenders.

Equipment Needed: Two large dummies and two small hand-shields.

Description: Two pairs of lines are formed. One line of each pair is designated the post blocker line. Another line is designated the lead blocker line. One dummy holder positions his dummy on the outside shade of the post blocker. The other dummy holder stands to the inside in a ready position. The blockers execute the techniques of the post-lead combination. Once the blockers begin to drive the dummy, the second dummy holder steps forward for the next pair of blockers. The blockers drive the dummy until the whistle is sounded. The next pair is immediately ready to go on the next drill repetition. One set of blockers practices against an anchor defender. One set of blockers practices against an inside stunt defender.

Coaching Points:

- The coach checks for the proper technique of the post blocker and lead blocker.

- The lead blocker must get his hip to contact the hip of the post blocker.

- The dummy must be blocked on a vertical path.

- The lead blocker must read the inside stunt and go up on the linebacker using the proper technique with the outside arm free.

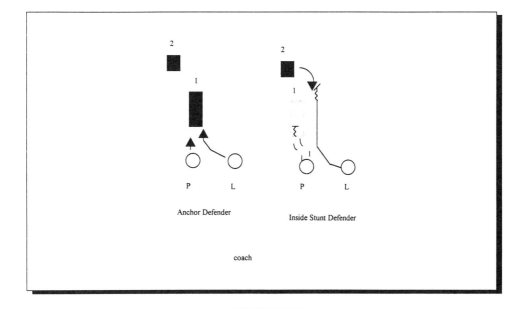

Drill #92: Sally Run-Pass Side Drill with Stunt

Objective: To incorporate the pass and run side blocking with the quarterback and ball carrier on the Sally play versus a playside stunt.

Equipment Needed: Football, four cones, one small hand-shield, and two large dummies.

Description: The run blocking side guard and the center perform their appropriate Sally block techniques for a Sally play to the right. The pass blocking side executes their proper techniques on the Sally play to the right. The quarterback takes the snap and executes his proper technique on the Sally play. The ball carrier executes his proper technique from the wingback position. The backup quarterback stands at the designated position and flashes a number to the quarterback. The quarterback is required to determine the number after handing off to the ball carrier. The coach may vary the defense to which the Sally is run. The drill is flipped for the Sally play to the left.

Coaching Points:

- The coach checks to see if the ball carrier hits the line of scrimmage with his shoulders square.

- The coach checks to see if the center attacks the large dummy with an aggressive pass protection technique and passes the weak stunting nose to the guard.

- The coach checks to see if the run side guard makes a 6 inch lateral step on the snap and takes over the nose man in the "A" gap.

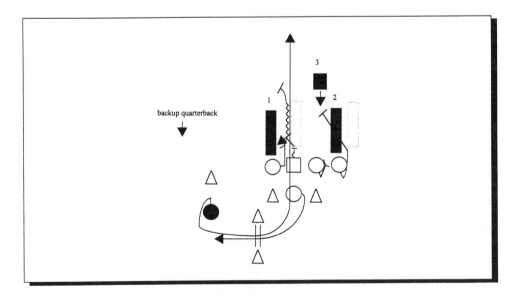

Drill #93: Quarterback Bootleg Drill

Objective: To teach the quarterback to look for the free safety on the bootleg/waggle.

Equipment Needed: Football, two barrels, and one large dummy.

Description: The quarterback takes the snap and fakes the buck sweep. The backs make good fakes and the quarterback gains depth to 8 yards and squares himself to the line of scrimmage between the barrels. The coach provides a read to the quarterback by going with the halfback fake or hanging in the middle.

Coaching Points:

- The quarterback turns his head to look at the halfback on the fake before bootlegging.

- The quarterback verbally yells flat or post in reaction to the movement of the coach. If the coach goes with the fake, the quarterback yells post, indicating he will throw the post route.

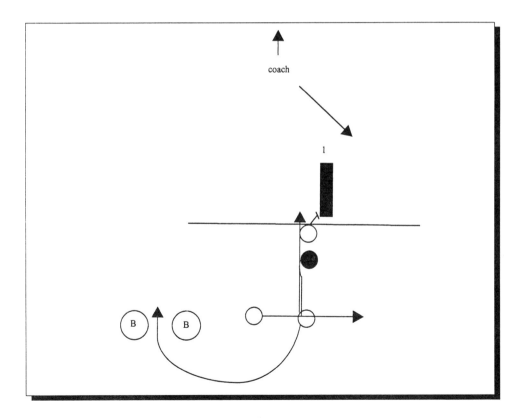

Drill #94: Sally Run-Pass Side Drill with Stunt

Objective: To incorporate the pass and run side blocking with the quarterback and ball carrier on the Sally play.

Equipment Needed: Football, four cones, two small hand-shields, and two large dummies.

Description: The run blocking side guard and the center perform their appropriate Sally block techniques for a Sally play to the right. The pass blocking side executes their proper techniques on the Sally play to the right. The quarterback takes the snap and executes his proper technique on the Sally play. The ball carrier executes his proper technique from the wingback position. The backup quarterback stands at the designated position and flashes a number to the quarterback. The quarterback is required to determine the number after handing off to the ball carrier. The coach may vary the defense to which the Saily is run. The drill is flipped for the Sally play to the left.

Coaching Points:

- The coach checks to see if the ball carrier hits the line of scrimmage with his shoulders square.

- The coach checks to see if the center attacks the large dummy with an aggressive pass protection technique and passes the weak stunting nose to the guard.

- The coach checks to see if the run side guard makes a 6 inch lateral step on the snap and takes over the nose man in the "A" gap.

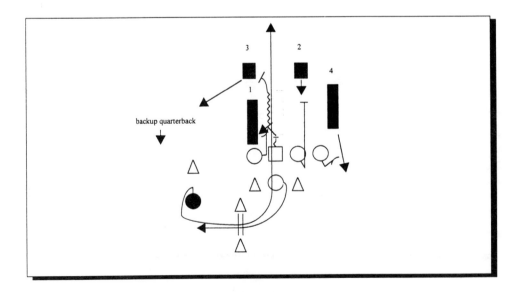

Drill #95: Buck Sweep Chute Drill

Objective: To incorporate the position techniques for the buck sweep.

Equipment Needed: 5 man chute, three cones, four shields and two large dummies.

Description: Two large dummies are laid on the ground as shown. Four hand shield-holders are positioned as shown. The individual position players execute their proper technique for the buck sweep. The backside tackle cuts off and breaks to the alley downfield. The backside guard sweep pulls to wall the pursuit. The center fires off. The playside guard sweep pulls to execute a hammer block. The playside tackle executes a down block. The drill is flipped over to run the buck sweep to the left.

Coaching Points:

- The coach makes sure the players align partially inside the chute.

- The coach makes sure the players, with the exception of the hammer guard, continue downfield for 15 yards.

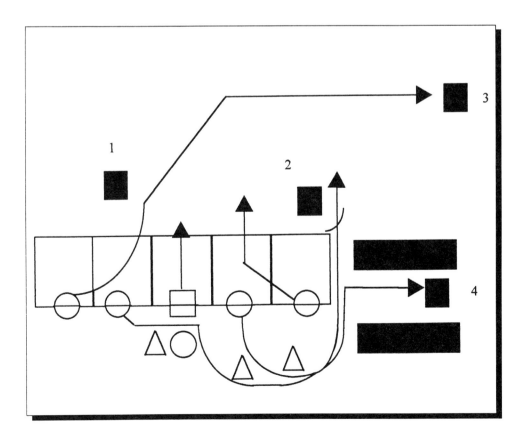

Drill #96: Shoulder Block Drive Drill

Objective: To combine the upper body technique of a shoulder block with the proper footwork.

Equipment Needed: Hand-held small shields.

Description: Players align in front of the available shield-holders. The shield-holders crouch so that the shield is held at knee level. The blocker pushes off his left foot and steps with his right foot. The following step of the push foot drives the inside shoulder to the face of the shield. The shoulder lifts the shield. The blocker should knock the shield-holder backward. The blocker pinches the shield with his neck and shoulder. The inside arm finishes the block with a punch to lift the shield.

Coaching Point:

- The shield holder must be driven upfield on a vertical path.

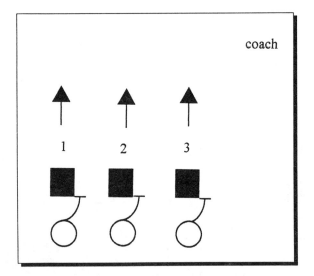

Drill #97: Bag Run Drill

Objective: To improve agility and footwork.

Equipment Needed: Five large blocking dummies, footballs.

Description: The dummies are laid on the ground one yard apart across a designated yard line. The players form a row along the yard line next to the first dummy. On the coach's signal, the first player shuffles laterally over the dummies, keeping his head up and his shoulders parallel to the yard line. As the player steps over the last dummy, the coach either passes the ball or rolls it on the ground to simulate a fumble. The player catches the pass or recovers the loose ball, returns it to the coach, and goes to the end of the row.

Coaching Points:

- The coach may tell players to move forward or backward over the dummies rather than sideways.

- Players should keep their center of gravity low to help maintain their balance.

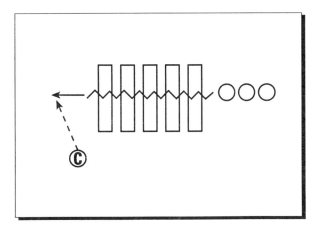

Drill #98: Push Starts

Objective: To practice pushing off the foot opposite the direction of the start.

Equipment Needed: 6 cones.

Description: The linemen are stationed in two lines. The cones are positioned as shown 5 yards from the starting point of the corresponding line. The drill is divided into three phases. The first phase is straight ahead starts. Each lineman drives off the inside foot and sprints to cone number one and jogs around behind the cones to return to the line. The athletes rotate until each athlete has push started off to each of the six cones, getting the opportunity to push off both the right and left foot.

Coaching Points:

- The athlete should be reminded to place his weight on his inside foot.

- The athlete should be encouraged to throw his hands forward in a simulated punch as he pushes off the push foot.

- The coach checks for mastery by observing the length of the first step. The push will result in a four to six inch stride with the ball of the lead foot hitting the ground.

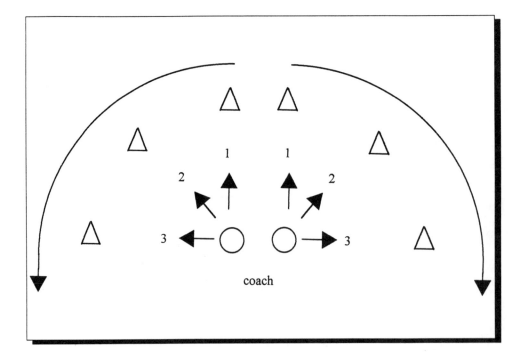

Drill 99: Post-Lead Blocker Drill

Objective: To combine the technique of the post block and the lead block of a double team combination.

Equipment Needed: Two large dummies.

Description: Two lines are formed. One line is designated the post blocker line. Another line is designated the lead blocker line. One dummy holder positions his dummy on the outside shade of the post blocker. The other dummy holder stands to the inside in a ready position. The blockers execute the techniques of the post-lead combination. Once the blockers begin to drive the dummy, the second dummy holder steps forward for the next pair of blockers. The blockers drive the dummy until the whistle is sounded. The next pair is immediately ready to go on the next drill repetition.

Coaching Points:

- The coach checks for the proper technique of the post blocker and lead blocker.

- The lead blocker must get his hip to contact the hip of the post blocker.

- The dummy must be blocked on a vertical path.

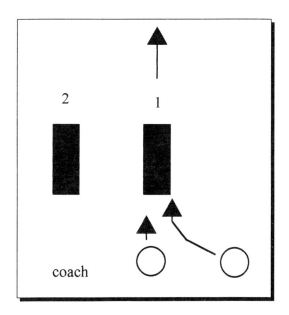

Drill #100: Anchor Sled Trap Drill

Objective: To reinforce the pull right-hit right and pull left-hit left trap maxim.

Equipment Needed: Five man sled anchored by metal stakes.

Description: The linemen are positioned all facing in one direction. The linemen are positioned five yards from the sled. The linemen push off the outside foot and attack the sled with the proper shoulder. The sled is lifted up by the simultaneous contact of the linemen. The linemen quickly back off the sled and move full speed in the direction opposite the shoulder used to contact the sled. The direction of the linemen is switched and the drill is repeated.

Coaching Points:

- The linemen quickly move off the sled at the highest point of the sled's lift.

- The coach stands behind the sled to ensure that the linemen have their heads up at the moment of contact.

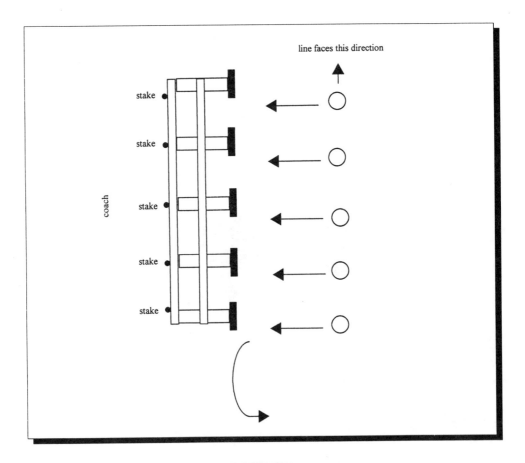

Drill #101: Post-Area Blocker Drill

Objective: To develop post blocking and area blocking skills against a slant defender.

Equipment: Two large dummies.

Description: Two lines are formed. The athlete practices area blocking straight ahead. The coach signals the dummy holder to step right or left while holding the dummy square to the line of scrimmage. The post blocker attacks the dummy straight on and swings his tail toward the step of the dummy holder in order to maintain head-on leverage. The coach randomly directs the dummy holder right and left. The coach also may direct the dummy holder to remain head-up on the blocker. The blocker drives the dummy upfield until the coach sounds the whistle.

Coaching Points:

- The coach observes the length of the blocker's first step.

- The athlete must get his buttocks around and drive the slanting dummy upfield.

- The athlete must not swing his buttocks opposite the direction of the slant defender.

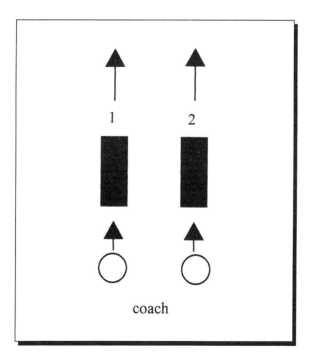

Harold R. "Tubby" Raymond is the head football coach at the University of Delaware—a position he has held since 1966. In that period, Raymond has led the Blue Hens to extraordinary accomplishments, including three national championships (1971, 1972 and 1979), 12 Lambert Cup Trophies, 13 NCAA playoff appearances, five Yankee Conference titles, and over 250 wins.

A 1950 graduate of the University of Michigan where he played both football and baseball for the Wolverines, Raymond has been honored numerous times for his coaching efforts, including being named NCAA Division II Coach of the year four times. A past president of the American Football Coaches Association, Raymond is widely renowned as one of the most outstanding football strategists in the history of the game.

Raymond has three children and eight grandchildren. Currently, he resides in Landerberg, Pennsylvania with his wife, Diane, and their daughter, Michelle.

Ted Kempski is the offensive coordinator for the University of Delaware football team. The starting quarterback on the 1961 and 1962 Blue Hen football teams, Kempski retuned to his alma mater in 1968 to coach the offensive backfield. In his 29 seasons on Tubby Raymond's staff, Kempski is credited with playing a key role in helping Delaware maintain its status as one of the premier rushing and total offense powerhouses in the nation.

Regarded as an exceptional teacher of football fundamentals, Kempski has helped three Blue Hen running backs become All-Americans—fullbacks Chuck Hall and Daryl Brown, and halfback Gardy Kahoe. A native of Wilmington, Delaware, where he was a multi-sport star in high school, Kempski currently resides in Elkton, Maryland with his wife Cathy. They have a son, Dan, and four grandchildren, Courtney, Katie, John and Zachary.